# THE AMERICAN PAINT HORSE

By Rachel Grack

Consultant:
Dr. Emily Leuthner
DVM, MS, DACVIM
Country View Veterinary Service
Oregon, Wisc.

BELLWETHER MEDIA • MINNEAPOLIS, MN

Jump into the cockpit and take flight with Pilot Books. Your journey will take you on high-energy adventures as you learn about all that is wild, weird, fascinating, and fun!

This edition first published in 2012 by Bellwether Media, Inc.

No part of this publication may be reproduced in whole or in part without written permission of the publisher. For information regarding permission, write to Bellwether Media, Inc., Attention: Permissions Department, 5357 Penn Avenue South, Minneapolis, MN 55419.

Library of Congress Cataloging-in-Publication Data

Koestler-Grack, Rachel A., 1973-
   The American paint horse / by Rachel Grack.
      p. cm. – (Pilot books. Horse breed roundup)
   Includes bibliographical references and index.
   Summary: "Engaging images accompany information about the American Paint Horse. The combination of high-interest subject matter and narrative text is intended for students in grades 3 through 7"–Provided by publisher.
   ISBN 978-1-60014-652-7 (hardcover : alk. paper)
   1.  American paint horse–Juvenile literature.  I. Title.
SF293.A47K64 2012
636.1'3–dc22                               2011010409

Printed in the United States of America, North Mankato, MN.

080111      1187

# CONTENTS

# The American Paint Horse

The crowd is hushed in anticipation. Suddenly, a horse and rider burst into the arena. The rider directs her horse as it weaves around three barrels at full speed. The event is barrel racing, and the competitor is an American Paint Horse. It's no surprise when this team finishes the course in record time. The American Paint Horse is a favorite at the **rodeo**!

Multicolored horses are known as **pintos**. The American Paint Horse is a specific breed of pinto. They are often called Paints. The American Paint Horse Association (APHA) **registers** young Paints. A Paint must have one parent that is an American Paint Horse. The other parent can be an American Paint Horse, American Quarter Horse, or Thoroughbred.

**A Spanish Name**
"Pinto" comes from pintado, which is Spanish for "painted."

American Paint Horses stand between 14 and 16 **hands** at the **withers**. Each hand equals 4 inches (10.2 centimeters), making Paints about 60 inches (152 centimeters) tall. Paints have muscular bodies with broad chests and powerful legs. This makes them good **stock horses**. Paints are suited to many different kinds of work because of their intelligence and calm **temperament**. Paints are happy to help!

All Paints are a combination of white and a shade of black or brown. Paints can also have more unique coats. The perlino coat looks cream-colored, but when you look closely, you can see faint white markings. The blue roan coat is a blend of white and black hairs. This makes the horse look blue!

blue roan

An American Paint Horse has one of three different coat patterns. These patterns are tobiano, overo, and tovero. Tobiano coats have large dark patches and large white patches. A Paint with a tobiano coat usually has four white legs. Overo coats have bigger dark patches than white patches. Dark patches often stretch across the back. Paints with overo coats have at least one leg that is dark in color, and often all four legs are dark. Tovero coats are mostly white, except for a small amount of color on the ears, mouth, chest, neck, or back.

American Paint Horse Coat Patterns

tobiano

overo

tovero

**Bald Horses?**
A Paint with an overo coat usually has a white face. A horse with a white face is sometimes called a bald-faced horse!

# An Ancient Origin

Multicolored horses have roamed the earth for thousands of years. Around 400 BCE, Egyptians drew them on the walls of tombs. The wandering tribes of the Gobi Desert in Asia also drew multicolored horses. They passed down stories about these colorful creatures for many generations.

Around 500 CE, the **Huns** rode multicolored horses from Asia into Europe when they invaded the Roman Empire. These horses became popular in and around Spain. By 700 CE, Spain had hundreds of horses with both tobiano and overo coats. Multicolored horses were prized among rich Europeans.

Spanish explorers set sail for the Americas in the 1500s. They brought horses along with them on their voyages. Some of the horses were multicolored. In 1519, Hernán Cortés and his crew landed in Mexico. The explorers rode the first multicolored horses onto North American soil.

Hernán Cortés

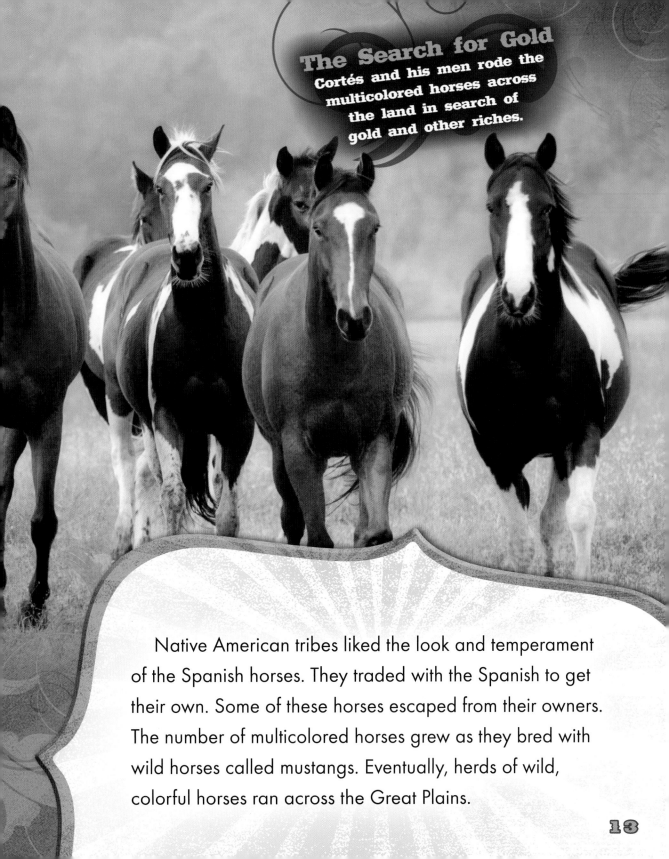

## The Search for Gold

Cortés and his men rode the multicolored horses across the land in search of gold and other riches.

Native American tribes liked the look and temperament of the Spanish horses. They traded with the Spanish to get their own. Some of these horses escaped from their owners. The number of multicolored horses grew as they bred with wild horses called mustangs. Eventually, herds of wild, colorful horses ran across the Great Plains.

The coats of multicolored horses provided **camouflage**. Native Americans quickly realized this was a great advantage in hunting and warfare. The horses helped them hide in woods, brush, and snow. They rode different colored horses depending on the season.

For many years, multicolored horses were called by different names. In 1965, a group of people began calling certain multicolored horses American Paint Horses. The group set **breed standards** and formed the American Paint Horse Association (APHA).

## Medicine Hats

Some Native Americans believed that certain multicolored horses held magical powers. The Comanche and the Cheyenne especially admired horses known as Medicine Hats. These horses are mostly white, with color only over the ears and across the chest. The dark chest looks like a shield protecting the horse. Only a Native American who proved himself to be a great warrior could ride a Medicine Hat.

# Ranches, Shows, and Competitions

American Paint Horses are strong, fast, and gentle. These traits make them excellent workers and racers. Many ranches use Paints to herd cattle, pull wagons, and do other work. Some Paints compete in horse races. Many are fast enough to beat Thoroughbreds and American Quarter Horses!

Paints have been favorite rodeo horses since the days of the Wild West. They are stars of the **show ring**. In barrel racing, a rider leads a horse around three barrels. The barrels are spaced in a triangle and are 60 to 105 feet (18 to 32 meters) apart. The speed and intelligence of Paints often help them win this event. Paints are also tough competitors in the Western pleasure **class**. In this class, horses are judged on how they perform certain **gaits**.

barrel racing

# Famous American Paint Horses

## Fritz

Fritz is considered the first famous animal movie star. He was the horse of early 1900s film star William Hart. Fritz performed many dangerous stunts in his movies. He jumped through windows and over fires. On one occasion, he jumped off a 12-foot (3.7-meter) cliff. When he landed, he fell over and pretended to be hurt. Fans of Fritz wrote him letters and even sent him sugar cubes to eat!

## Powder Charge

Powder Charge was a chestnut tobiano Paint that raced during the 1960s and 1970s. He came from a long line of racing horses. He raced against Thoroughbreds, American Quarter Horses, Appaloosas, and other Paints. He won all but two of the races he entered. In 1967, he was awarded the Register of Merit in Racing. Although he died young in 1972, he had many foals that became racing champions.

Some competitions are only for Paints. Every year, the APHA holds two World Championship Paint Horse Shows in Fort Worth, Texas. One show is for young riders and one is for adults. Competitions include speed and cattle events, team challenges, and **halter**. Riders are judged on **horsemanship**. Young riders show off their horse knowledge by competing in a **hippology** contest.

About 3,800 horses were registered when the APHA first formed. Since then, more than 981,000 Paints have been registered. The American Paint Horse is the fifth most-registered breed in the world. It is one of the fastest-growing breeds, with more than 30,000 **foals** registered each year. The beauty and calm nature of the American Paint Horse make the breed a favorite of many horse lovers!

# Glossary

**breed standards—** the physical characteristics of a breed; horses must meet breed standards to be recognized by the official breed organization.

**camouflage—**coloring and patterns that hide an animal by making it look like its surroundings

**class—**a category of competition at a horse show

**foals—**young horses; foals are under one year old.

**gaits—**the ways in which a horse moves; walking, trotting, and cantering are examples of gaits.

**halter—**an event at a horse show; during halter, owners lead their horses into a show ring to be inspected by judges.

**hands—**the units used to measure the height of a horse; one hand is equal to 4 inches (10.2 centimeters).

**hippology—**the study of horses

**horsemanship—**the riding, training, and handling of horses

**Huns—**an ancient group of people that lived in central Asia; the Huns invaded and conquered large parts of Europe.

**pintos—**multicolored horses; most horses with coats that have white and one other color can be called pintos.

**registers—**makes record of; owners register their horses with official breed organizations.

**rodeo—**a competition in which riders perform various skills on horses

**show ring—**the ring where horses compete and are displayed at a horse show

**stock horses—**horses suited for work, especially with cattle

**temperament—**personality or nature; the American Paint Horse has a calm temperament.

**withers—**the ridge between the shoulder blades of a horse

# To Learn More

## At the Library

Denniston, David. *The American Paint Horse*. Mankato, Minn.: Capstone Press, 2005.

Stone, Lynn M. *Paint Horses*. Vero Beach, Fla.: Rourke Pub., 2008.

Van Cleaf, Kristin. *American Paint Horses*. Edina, Minn.: ABDO Pub., 2006.

## On the Web

Learning more about American Paint Horses is as easy as 1, 2, 3.

1. Go to www.factsurfer.com.

2. Enter "American Paint Horses" into the search box.

3. Click the "Surf" button and you will see a list of related Web sites.

With factsurfer.com, finding more information is just a click away.

# Index

The images in this book are reproduced through the courtesy of: Henry Wilson, front cover, pp. 6, 8 (left & middle), 18-19; Mark J. Barrett / KimballStock, pp. 4-5, 12-13; Lisa Dugger, p. 7; Stephanie / jumpinghooves, p. 8 (right); Ron Kimball / KimballStock, p. 9; Carol Walker / naturepl.com, pp. 10-11; Getty Images, p. 12; Nancy G Western Photography / Nancy Greifenhagen / Alamy, p. 14; Diane Garcia, pp. 16-17; Barbara Tripp, pp. 20-21.